The Poetry of Bliss Carman

Volume XIII - Pipes of Pan No IV. Songs From a Northern Garden

William Bliss Carman was born in Fredericton, in New Brunswick on April 15th 1861. He was educated at Fredericton Collegiate School before moving to the University of New Brunswick, obtaining his B.A. there in 1881. As is common with so many writers his first published piece was for the University magazine and for Carman that was in 1879.

After several years editing various magazines and periodicals Carman first published a poetry volume in 1893 with Low Tide on Grand Pré. There was no Canadian company prepared to publish and when an American company did so it went bankrupt.

The following year was decidedly better. His partnership with the American poet Richard Hovey had given birth to Songs of Vagabondia. It was an immediate success.

That success prompted the Boston firm, Stone & Kimball, to reissue Low Tide on Grand Pré and to hire Carman as the editor of its literary journal, The Chapbook.

Carman brought out, in 1895, Behind the Arras, a somewhat more serious and philosophical work centered on the premise of a long meditation, using the speaker's house and its many rooms, as a symbol of life and the choices to be made.

In 1896 Carman met Mrs Mary Perry King, who rapidly became patron, adviser and sometime lover. She also became his writing collaborator on two verse dramas.

In 1897 Carman published Ballad of Lost Haven, and in 1898, By the Aurelian Wall, the title poem itself was an elegy to John Keats and the book was a collection of formal elegies.

As the century turned Carman was hard at work on a five-volume set of poetry "Pans Pipes". The excellence of a number of these poems did much to install Carman as the most noted of Canadian Poets and eventually their own Poet Laureate.

In 1912 the final work in the Vagabondia series was published. Richard Hovey had died in 1900 and so this last work was purely Carman's. It has a distinct elegiac tone as if remembering the past works themselves.

On October 28th, 1921 Carman was honored by the newly-formed Canadian Authors' Association where he was crowned Canada's Poet Laureate with a wreath of maple leaves.

William Bliss Carman died of a brain hemorrhage at the age of 68 in New Canaan on the 8th June, 1929.

Index of Contents

OUR LADY OF THE RAIN

Across the purple valleys,
Along the misty hills,
By murmur-haunted rivers
And silver-gurgling rills,
By woodland, swamp and barren,
By road and field and plain,
Arrives the Green Enchantress,
Our Lady of the Rain.

Her pure and mystic planet
Is lighted in the west;
In ashe-rose and lilac
Of melting evening dressed.
With golden threads of sunset
Inwoven in her gown,
With glamour of the springtime
She has bewitched the town.

Her look is soft with dreaming
On old forgotten years;
Her eyes are grave and tender
With unpermitted tears;
For she has known the sorrows
Of all this weary earth,
Yet ever brings it gladness,
Retrieval and new birth.

And when her splendid pageant,
Sidereal and slow,

With teeming stir and import
Sweeps up from line to snow.
There's not an easer mortal
But would arise and make
Some orave unoromisea venture
For her immortal sake.

For no man knows what power
Is sleeping in the seed,
What destiny may slumber
Within the smallest deed.
In calm no fret can hurry,
Nor any fear detain,
She brings our own to meet us
Our Lady of the Rain.

She saw the red clay moulded
And quickened into man;
The sweetness of her spirit
Within his pulses ran;
The ardour of her being
Was in his veins like fire,
The unreluctant passion,
The unallayed desire.

'Twas she who brought rejoicing
To Babylon and Ur.
To Carthage and to Sidon
Men came to worship her.
Her soft spring rites were honoured
At Argolis and Troy,
And dark Caldean women
Gave thanks to her for joy.

With cheer and exaltation
With hope for all things born,
To hearten the disheartened,
To solace the forlorn,
Too gentle and all-seeing
For judgment or disdain,
She comes with loving kindness
Our Lady of the Rain.

With magical resurgence
For all the sons of men
She crosses winter's frontier,
They know not whence nor when.
Yet silently as sunlight

Along the forest floor
Her step is on the threshold,
Her shadow at the door.

On many a lonely clearing
Among the timbered hills
She calls across the distance,
Until the twilight fills
With voice of loosened waters,
And from the marshy ground
The frogs begin refilling
Their flutes with joyous sound.

Then note by note is lifted
The chorus clear and shrill.
And all who hear her summons
Must answer to her will;
For she will not abandon
The old Pandean strain
That called the world from chaos —
Our Lady of the Rain.

And still her wondrous music
Comes up with early spring,
And meadowland and woodland
With silver wildness ring;
The sparrow by the roadside,
The wind among the reeds,
Whoever hears that piping
Must follow where it leads.

Though no man knows the reason,
Nor how the rumour spread,
Through canyon-streeted cities
Her message has been sped;
And some forgotten longing
To hear a bluebird sing
Bids folk from open windows
Look forth and it is spring.

Come out into the sunshine,
You dwellers of the town,
Put by your anxious dolors,
And cast your sorrows down.
O, starved and pampered people,
How futile is your gain!
Behold, there comes to heal you
Our Lady of the Rain.

Go where the buds are breaking
Upon the cherry bough,
And the strong sap is mounting
In every tree-trunk now;
Where orchards are in blossom
On every spray and spire,
Go hear the orioles whistle
And pass like flecks of fire.

Go find the first arbutus
Within the piney wood,
And learn from that shy dweller
How sweet is solitude;
Go listen to the white-throat
In some remote ravine
Rehearse in tranquil patience
His ecstasy serene.

Go down along the beaches
And borders of the sea,
When golden morning kindles
That blue immensity,
And watch the white sails settle
Below the curving rim
Of this frail vast of colour,
Diaphanous and dim.

Go watch by brimming river
Or reedy-marged lagoon
The wild geese row their galley
Across the rising moon,
That comes up like a bubble
Out of the black fir-trees,
And ask what mind invented
Such miracles as these.

Who came when we were sleeping
And wrought this deathless lure,
This vivid vernal wonder
Improbable and sure?
Where Algol and Bootes
Mark their enormous range,
What seraph passed in power
To touch the world with change?

What love's unerring purpose
Reveals itself anew

In these mysterious transports
Of tone and shape and hue?
Doubt not the selfsame impulse
Throbs in thy restless side,
Craves at the gates of being,
And would not be denied.

Be thou the west wind's brother,
And kin to bird and tree,
The soul of spring may utter
Her oracles to thee;
Her breath shall give thee courage,
Her tan shall touch thy cheek,
The words of sainted lovers
Be given thee to speak.

Fear not the mighty instinct,
The great Aprilian Creed;
The House of Spring is open
And furnished for thy need.
But fear the little wisdom,
The paltry doubt and vain,
And trust without misgiving
Our Lady of the Rain.

What foot would fail to meet her,
And who would stay indoor,
When April in her glory
Comes triumphing once more
When adder-tongue and tulip
Put on their coats of gold,
And all the world goes love-mad
For beauty as of old?

At every year's returning
The swallows will be here,
The stalls be gay with jonquils,
The dogwood re-appear;
And up from the south westward
Come back to us again
With sorceries of gladness
Our Lady of the Rain.

IN A GRAND PRÉ GARDEN

In a garden over Grand Pre, dewy in the morning sun,

Here in earliest September with the summer nearly done,
Musing on the lovely world and all its beauties, one by one!

Bluets, marigolds, and asters, scarlet poppies, purple phlox,
Who knows where the key is hidden to those frail yet perfect locks
In the tacit doors of being where the soul stands still and knocks?

There is Blomidon's blue sea-wall, set to guard the turbid straits
Where the racing tides have entry; but who keeps for us the gates
In the mighty range of silence where man's spirit calls and waits?

Where is Glooscaap? There's a legend of that saviour of the West,
The benign one, whose all-wisdom loved beasts well, though men the best,
Whom the tribes of Minas leaned on, and their villages had rest.

Once the lodges were defenceless, all the warriors being gone
On a hunting or adventure. Like a panther on a fawn,
On the helpless stole a war-band, ambushed to attack at dawn.

But with night came Glooscaap. Sleeping he surprised them; waved his bow;
Through the summer leaves descended a great frost, as white as snow;
Sealed their slumber to eternal peace and stillness, long ago.

Then a miracle. Among them, while still death undid their thews,
Slept a captive with her children. Such the magic he could use,
She arose unharmed with morning, and departing, told the news.

He, too, when the mighty Beaver had the country for his pond,
All the way from the Pereau here to Bass River and beyond,
Stoned the rascal; drained the Basin; routed out that vagabond.

You can see yourself Five Islands Glooscaap flung at him that day,
When from Blomidon to Sharp he tore the Beaver's dam away,
Cleared the channel, and the waters thundered out into the bay.

(Do we idle, little children? Ah, well, there is hope, maybe,
In mere beauty which enraptures just such ne'er-do-wells as we!
I must go and pick my apples. Malyn will be calling me!)

Here he left us see the orchards, red and gold in every tree!
All the land from Gaspereau to Portapique and Cheverie,
All the garden lands of Minas and a passage out to sea.

You can watch the white-sailed vessels through the meadows wind and creep.
All day long the pleasant sunshine, and at night the starry sleep,
While the labouring tides that rest not have their business with the deep!

So I get my myth and legend of a breaker-down of bars,

Putting gateways in the mountains with their thousand-year-old scars,
That the daring and the dauntless might steer outward by the stars.

So my demiurgic hero lays a frost on all our fears.
Dead the grisly superstition, dead the bigotry of years,
Dead the tales that frighten children, when the pure white light appears.

Thus did Glooscaap of the mountains. What doth Balder of the flowers,
Balder, the white lord of April, who comes back amid the showers
And the sunshine to the Northland to revive this earth of ours?

First, how came my garden, where untimely not a leaf may wilt?
For a thousand years the currents trenched the rock and wheeled the silt,
Dredged and filled and smoothed and levelled, toiling that it might be built.

For the moon pulled and the sun pushed on the derrick of the tide;
And a great wind heaved and blustered, swung the weight round with a stride,
Mining tons of red detritus out of the old mountain side,

Bore them down and laid them even by the mouth of stream and rill
For the quiet lowly doorstep, for cemented joist and sill
Of our Grand Pre, where the cattle lead their shadows or lie still.

So my garden floor was founded by the labouring frugal sea,
Deep and virginal as Eden, for the flowers that were to be,
All for my great drowsy poppies and my marigolds and me.

Who had guessed the unsubstantial end and outcome of such toil,
These, the children of a summer, whom a breath of frost would foil,
I, almost as faint and fleeting as my brothers of the soil?

Did those vague and drafty sea-tides, as they journeyed, feel the surge
Of the prisoned life that filled them seven times full from verge to verge,
Mounting to some far achievement where its ardour might emerge?

Are they blinder of a purpose in their courses fixed and sure,
Those sea arteries whose heavings throb through Nature's vesture,
Than my heart's frail valves and hinges which so perilously endure?

Do I say to it, "Give over!" Can I will, and it will cease?
Nay, it stops but with destruction; knows no respite nor release.

I, who did not start its pulses, cannot bid them be at peace.
Thus the great deep, framed and fashioned to a thought beyond its own,
Rocked by tides that race or sleep without its will from zone to zone,

Setting door-stones for a people in a century unknown,
Sifted for me and my poppies the red earth we love so well.

Gently there, my fine logician, brooding in your lone grey cell!

Was it all for our contentment such a miracle befell?
No; because my drowsy poppies and my marigolds and I
Have this human need in common, nodding as the wind goes by;

There is that supreme within us no one life can satisfy.
With their innocent grave faces lifted up to meet my own,
They are but the stranger people, swarthy children of the sun,

Gypsies tenting at our door to vanish ere the year is done.
(How we idle, little children! Still our best of tasks may be,
From distraction and from discord without baseness to get free.

I must go and pick my apples. Malyn will be calling me!)
Humbly, then, most humbly ever, little brothers of the grass,
With Aloha at your doorways I salute you as you pass,

I who wear the mortal vesture, as our custom ever was.
Known for kindred by the habit, by the tanned and crimson stain,
Earthlings in the garb ensanguined just so long as we remain,

You for days and I for seasons mystics by the common strain,
Till we tread the virgin threshold of a great moon red and low,
Clean and joyous while we tarry, and uncraven when we go

From the rooftree of the rain-wind and the broad eaves of the snow.
And this thing called life, which frets us like a fever without name,
Soul of man and seed of poppy no mortality can tame,

Smouldering at the core of beauty till it breaks in perfect flame,
What it is I know not; only I know they and I are one,
By the lure that bids us linger in the great House of the Sun,

By the fervour that sustains us at the door we cannot shun.
From a little wider prospect, I survey their bright domain;
On a rounder dim horizon, I behold the ploughman rain;

All I have and hold so lightly, they will perish to attain.
Waking at the word of April with the South Wind at her heels,
We await the revelation locked beneath the four great seals,

Ice and snow and dark and silence, where the Northern search-light wheels.
Waiting till our Brother Balder walks the lovely earth once more,
With the robin in the fir-top, with the rain-wind at the door,
With the old unwearied gladness to revive us and restore,

We abide the raptured moment, with the patience of a stone,

Like ephemera our kindred, transmigrant from zone to zone,
To that last fine state of being where they live on joy alone.

O great Glooscaap and kind Balder, born of human heart's desire,
When earth's need took shape and substance, and the impulse to aspire
Passed among the new-made peoples, touching the red clay with fire,

By the myth and might of beauty, lead us and allure us still,
Past the open door of wonder and oblivion's granite sill,
Past the curtain of the sunset in the portals of the hill,

To new provinces of wisdom, sailless latitudes of soul.
I for one must keep the splendid faith in good your lives extol,
Well assured the love you lived by is my being's source and goal.

Fearless when the will bids "Venture," or the sleepless mind bids "Know,"
Here among my lowly neighbours blameless let me come and go,
Till I, too, receive the summons to the silent Tents of Snow.

In a garden over Grand Pré, bathed in the serenity
Of the early autumn sunlight, came these quiet thoughts to me,
While the wind went down the orchard to the dikes and out to sea.

(Idling yet? My flowery children, only far too well I see
How this day will glow forever in my life that is to be!
I must go and pick my apples. There is Malyn calling me!)

THE KEEPERS OF SILENCE

My hillside garden half-way up
The mountains from the purple sea,
Beholds the pomp of days go by
In summer's gorgeous pageantry.

I watch the shadows of the clouds
Stream over Grand Pré in the sun,
And the white fog seethe up and spill
Over the rim of Blomidon.

For past the mountains to the North,
Like a great caldron of the tides,
Is Fundy, boiling round their base,
And ever fuming up their sides.

Yet here within my valley world
No breath of all that tumult stirs;

The little orchards sleep in peace;
Forever dream the dark blue firs.

And while far up the gorges sweep
The silver legions of the showers,
I have communion with the grass
And conversation with the flowers.

More wonderful than human speech
Their dialect of silence is,
The simple Dorian of the fields,
So full of homely subtleties.

When the dark pansies nod to say
Good morning to the marigolds,
Their velvet taciturnity
Reveals as much as it withholds.

I always half expect to hear
Some hint of what they mean to do;
But never is their fine reserve
Betrayed beyond a smile or two.

Yet very well at times I seem
To understand their reticence,
And so, long since, I came to love
My little brothers by the fence.

Perhaps some August afternoon,
When earth is only half-aware,
They will unlock their heart for once,
How sad if I should not be there!

AT HOME AND ABROAD

My modest Northern garden
Is full of yellow flowers,
And quaking leaves and sunlight
And long noon hours.

It hangs upon the hillside
Above the little town;
And there in pleasant weather
You can look far down,

To the broad dikes of Grand Pre

Roamed over by the herds,
And the purple Minas water
Where fish the white sea-birds.

I watch the little vessels,
Where the slow rivers glide
Between the grassy orchards.
Come in upon the tide.

For daily there accomplished
Is the sea's legerdemain,
To fill the land with rivers
And empty it again.

Before you lies North Mountain,
Built like a long sea-wall
A wonder in blue summer
And in the crimson fall.

The sea-fogs cloud and mantle
Along its fir-dark crest,
While under it the fruit-lands
Have shelter and have rest.

And when the goblin moonlight
Loiters upon her round
Of valley, marsh and mountain
To bless my garden-ground,

(The harvest moon that lingers
Until her task is done,
And all the grain is ripened
For her great lord, the sun,)

I know that there due northward,
Under the polar star,
Sir Blomidon is fronting
Whatever storms there are.

I cannot see those features
I love so well by day,
Calmed by a thousand summers,
Scarred by the winter's play;

Yet there above the battle
Of the relentless tides,
Under the solemn starlight
He muses and abides.

And in the magic stillness,
The moonlight's ghostly gleam
Makes me its sylvan brother,
To rove the world a-dream.

That wayward and oblivious
Mortal I seem to be
Shall habit not forever
This garden by the sea.

Not Blomidon nor Grand Pre
Shall be his lasting home,
Nor all the Ardise country
Give room enough to roam.

Even to-night a little
He strays, and will not bide
The gossip of the flowers,
The rumour of the tide.

He must be forth and seeking,
Beyond this garden-ground,
The arm-in-arm companion
For whom the sun goes round.

And in the soft May weather
I walk with you again,
Where the terraces of Meudon
Look down upon the Seine.

KILLOOLEET

There's a wonderful woodland singer
In the North, called Killooleet,
That is to say Little Sweetvoice
In the tongue of the Milicete,

The tribe of the upper Wolaastook,
Who range that waterway
From the blue fir hills of its sources
To the fogs and tides of the bay.

All day long in the sunshine,
All night long through the rains,
On the grey wet cedar barrens

And the lonely blueberry plains,

You may hear Killooleet singing,
Hear his O sweet
(Then a grace-note, then the full cadence),
Killooleet, Killooleet, Killooleet!

Whenever you dip a paddle,
Or set a pole in the stream,
Killooleet marks the ripple,
Killooleet knows the gleam;

Killooleet gives you welcome,
Killooleet makes you free
With the great sweet wilderness freedom
That holds over land and sea.

You may slide your birch through the alders,
Or camp where the rapids brawl,
The first glad forest greeting
Will still be Killooleet's call.

Wherever you drive a tent-pin,
Or kindle a fire at night,
Killooleet comes to the ridge-pole,
Killooleet answers the light.

The dark may silence the warblers;
The heavy and thunderous hush
That comes before storm may stifle
The pure cool notes of the thrush;

The waning season may sober
Bobolink, bluebird, and quail ;
But Killooleet's stainless transport
Will not diminish nor fail.

Henceforth you shall love and fear not,
Remembering Killooleet's song
Haunting the wild waste places,
Deliberate, tranquil, and strong;

And so you shall come without cunning,
But wise in the simpler lore,
To the House of the Little Brothers,
And God will open the door.

MARSYAS

In the woods the timid creatures, reassured, approach and peer,
Half aware the charm's allurement they must follow as they hear
Is the first far-loo ked-for presage of the banishment of fear.

Silence falls upon the woodland, quiet settles on the plain;
Earth and air and the blue heaven, without harm or taint or stain,
Are restored to their old guise of large serenity again.

Thus the player at his piping in the early mode and grave
Took from Wisdom the inventress what the earth in bounty gave,
And therein to round completion put the beating heart and brave.

So, you artists and musicians, earth awaits perfection still;
Wisdom tarries by the brookside, beauty loiters on the hill,
For the love that shall reveal them with the yet undreamed-of skill.

Love be therefore all your passion, the one ardour that ye spend
To enhance the craft's achievement with signicance and trend,
Making faultless the wild strain that else were faulty to the end.

Love must lend the magic cadence that un-earthly dying fall
When the simple sweet earth-music takes us captive past recall,
And the loved one and the lover lose this world, nor care at all.

SYRINX

Once I saw (O breath of Summer!) in the azure prime of June,
When the Northland takes her joy and sets her wintered life in tune,
The soft wind come down the river, where a heron slept at noon;

Stir the ripening meadow-grasses, lift the lily-pads, and stray
Through the tall green ranks of rushes bowing to its ghostly sway;
Then I heard it, like a whisper of the world, take voice and say:

"Mortal by the wood-wind's murmur and the whisper of the stream,
I, who am the breath of grasses and the soul of Summer's dream,
Once was Syrinx, whom a great god loved and lost and made the theme

"Of his mournful minor music. Nay, I who had worn the guise
Which allured him, yet eluded, vanishing before his eyes,
When his heart held lonely commune, taking counsel to devise

"Some new solace for sad lovers that should give the spirit vent,

Lovelier than speech of mortals where the stricken soul is pent
And the longing gropes for language large enough for beauty's bent;

"When he drew the reeds and ranged them, rank by rank from low to shrill,
Bound them with the flax together I was inspiration still,
I was heartache crying through them, I was echo on the hill.

"And forever I am cadence, joyous, welling, sad or fond,
When the breath of god or mortal, breaking time's primeval bond,
Blows upon the mouths of wood and all the mellow throats respond.

"Not a flute, but I have hidden in its haunted hollow mould;
In the deep Sicilian twilight, when the shepherd piped to fold,
I have been the eerie calling of the Pan pipes rude and old;

"From the ivory monaulos, when the soft Egyptian stars
Sentried Cleopatra's gardens, through the open window-bars
I went forth, a splendid torment, o'er the dreaming nenuphars.

"In the silver-mounted laurel played by some Byzantine boy,
I was frenzy, when the throng night after night went mad for joy,
As the dancer Theodora made the Emperor her toy.

"In the boxwood bound with gold I drew my captives down the Nile,
To the love-feasts of Bubastis, lovers by the thousand file,
Willing converts to my love-call, children of the changeless smile.

"Babylonian Mylitta heard me keep the limpid tune,
When the lovers danced before her at the feast of the new moon,
Till the rosy flowers of beauty through her sacred groves were strewn.

"And Sidonian Astarte and the Asian Cypriote
Knew the large unhurried measure of my earth-sweet pagan rote,
When the dancing youths before them followed me from note to note.

"Where some lithe Bithynian flute-boy, nude and golden in the sun,
Set his red mouth to the twin pipes, I was in each pause and run,
When his manhood took the meaning of the love-notes one by one.

"And amid the fields of iris by the blue Ionian sea,
I was solemn-hearted sweetness and pure passion soon to be
In the dark-haired little maid who piped her budding melody.

"I was youth and love and rapture, I was madness in their veins,
Calling through the heats of Summer, calling in the soft Spring rains,
From the olive Phrygian hillsides and the deep Boeotian plains.

"I but blew, and mortals followed; I but breathed, and they were glad,

King and mendicant and sailor, courtesan and shepherd lad;
For there is no creed nor canon laid on music's myriad.

"Not a tribe nor race nor people born in darkest savagery,
Dwellers in the Afric forest or the islands of the sea,
But I wooed them from their war-drums made them gentle set them free.

"Silence fell upon the tam-tams throbbing terror through the night,
And the prayer-gongs ceased to conjure cowering villages with fright,
When my cool note, clear as morning, called them to a new delight.

"I, the breath of flute and oboe, golden wood and silver reed,
Put away their fear, and taught them with my love- tone to give heed,
When the love grew large within them, to the lovely spirit's need.

"Henceforth no mere frantic rhythm of beating foot and patting hand,
Nor monotonous marimba could suffice for soul's demand,
When Joy called her wayworn children and Peace wandered through the land.

"Love must build a better music than the strumming tambourine,
To ensphere his worlds of wonder, height and depth and space between,
Pleasure-lands for Soul, the lover, to preempt as his demesne.

"So he took the simple reed-note, as a dewdrop clear and round,
Blew it (magic of creation!) to the tenuous profound
Of sheer gladness, light and colour of the universe of sound.

"And there soars the shining structure, tone on tone as star on star,
Spheres of knowledge and of beauty, where love's compensations are,
And the plenitudes of spirit move to rhythm without a jar;

"Every impulse in its orbit swinging to the utmost range
Of the normal sweep of being, through unfathomed gulfs of change,

Poised, unswerved, and never finding aught unlovely or unstrange.

"When some dark Peruvian lover set the love-flute to his lip,
I was the new soft enchantment loosed upon the dusk, to slip
Through the trees and thrill the loved one from warm nape to finger-tip;

"Till she could not choose but follow where my player piped for her;
So I roused the love within her, set the gipsy pulse astir,
With my wild delicious pleading, strong as incense, fine as myrrh.

"When for love the Winnebago took his courting-flute and played
His wild theme for days together near the lodge-door of his maid,
I was ritual and rapture of the triumph he essayed.

"And my brown Malayan lovers pierce the living gold bamboo,
For the lone melodious accents of the wind to wander through,
While my haunting spirit tells them many a secret old and true.

"In the soft Sumatran pan-flute with its seven notes I plead;
I am help to the Marquesan in his slender scarlet reed;
From the immemorial East I draw my dark-eyed gipsy breed.

"Chukma, Dyak, Mahalaka, Papuan and Ashanti,
Hillmen from the Indian snows, canoemen from the Carib sea,
Tribesmen from the world's twelve corners, at my whisper come to me

"All the garlanded earth-children in their gala bright array,
Laughing like the leaves, or sighing like the grass-heads which I sway;
For my lure is swift to lead them, and my solace strong to stay.

"And the road must melt before them and their piping fill all lands,
Till a new world at their fluting like a magic flower expands,
And Soul's unexplored dominion is surrendered to their hands.

"Did not I, the woodbreath, calling, make thy mortal pulses ring,
And thy many-seasoned roof-tree with its dusty rafters sing?
Was not I the long sweet love-throb in the music-house of Spring?

"Think how all the golden willows and the maples crimson- keyed,
Kept the rare appointed season, flowering at the instant need,
When the wood-pipes gave my summons and the marshy flutes were freed!

Love be, then, in every heart-beat, when the year comes round to June,
And life reaches up to rapture, lingering on the perfect tune,
As this evening in your valley silvered by the early moon."

Thus I heard the voice of Syrinx, by the dreamy river shore,
Sift and cease, as one might pass through a large room and close the door;
And I knew myself a stranger on this lovely earth no more.

THE MAGIC FLUTE

Hear, O Syrinx, thou lost dryad! Marsyas, thou mortal, hear!
If to lovely and free spirits it is granted to draw near
And revisit the whole earth from some far-off and twilight sphere,

Like the limpid star of evening hanging o'er the dark hill brow,
Globed in light to touch this valley where a worshipper I bow,
O give heed, and of your wisdom help a mortal lover now!

All the while not a word from my sunflowers here on the hill.
And to-night when the stars over Blomidon flower and fill
The blue Northern garden of heaven, so pale and so still,
From the lordly king-aster Aldebaran there by the sill
Of the East, where the moonlight will enter, not one will fulfil
A lordlier lot than my sunflowers here on the hill.

So much for mere fact, mere impression. So much I portray
Of the atmosphere, colour, illusion of one autumn day,
In the little Acadian village above the Grand Pré;
Just the quiet of orchards and firs, where the sun had full sway,
And the river went trolling his soft wander-song to the bay,
While roseberry, aster, and sagaban tangled his way.
Be you their interpreter, reasoner; tell what they say,
These children of silence whose patient regard I portray.

You Londoner, walking in Bishopsgate, strolling the Strand,
Some morning in autumn afford, at a fruit-dealer's stand,
The leisure to look at his apples there ruddy and tanned.
Then ask, when he's smiling to serve you, if choice can command
A Gravenstein grown oversea on Canadian land.
(And just for the whim's sake, for once, you'll have no other brand!)
How teach you to tell them? Pick one, and with that in your hand,
Bethink you awhile as you turn again into the Strand.

"What if," you will say, so smooth in your hand it will lie,
So round and so firm, of so rich a red to the eye,
Like a dash of Fortuny, a tinge of some Indian dye,
While you turn it and toss, mark the bloom, ere you taste it and try,
"Now what if this grew where the same bright pavilion of sky
Is stretched o'er the valley and hillside he bids me descry,

The windless valley of peace, where the seasons go by,
And the river goes down through the orchards where long shadows lie!"
There's the fruit in your hand, in your ears is the roar of the street,
The pulse of an empire keeping its volume and beat,
Its sure come and go day and night, while we sleep or we eat.
Taste the apple, bite in to the juice; how abundant and sweet!
As sound as your own English heart, and wholesome as wheat.
There grow no such apples as that in your Bishopsgate street.

Or perhaps in St. Helen's Place, when your business is done
And the ledgers put by, you will think of the hundred and one
Commissions and errands to do; but what under the sun

Was that, so important? Ah, yes! the new books overrun
The old shelves. It is high time to order a new set begun.
Then off to the joiner's. You enter to see his plane run
With a long high shriek through the lumber he's working upon.
Then he turns from his shavings to query what you would have done.

But homeward 'tis you who make question. That song of the blade!
And the sharp sweet cry of the wood, what an answer it made!
What stories the joiner must hear, as he plies his clean trade,
Of all the wild life of the forest where long shadows wade
The untrodden moss, and the firs send a journeying shade
So slow through the valley so far from the song of his blade.

Come back to my orchards a moment. They're waiting for you.
How still are the little grey leaves where the pippins peep through!
The boughs where the ribstons hang red are half-breaking in two.
Above them September in magical soft Northern blue
Has woven the spell of her silence, like frost or like dew,
Yet warm as a poppy's red dream. When All Saints shall renew
The beauty of summer awhile, will their dreaming come true?
Ah, not of my Grand Pre they dream, nor your London and you!

Their life is their own, and the surge of it. All through the spring
They pushed forth their buds, and the rainbirds at twilight would sing.
They put forth their bloom, and the world was as fairy a thing
As a Japanese garden. Then midsummer came with a zing
And the clack of the locust; then fruit-time and coolness, to bring
This aftermath deep underfoot with its velvety spring.

And they all the while with the fatherly, motherly care,
Taking sap from the strength of the ground, taking sun from the air,
Taking chance of the frost and the worm, taking courage to dare,
Have given their life that the life might be goodly and fair
In their kind for the seasons to come, with good witness to bear
How the sturdy old race of the apples could give and not spare.
To-morrow the harvest begins. We shall rifle them there
Of the beautiful fruit of their bodies, the crown of their care.

How lovingly then shall the picker set hand to the bough!
Bid it yield, ere the seed come to earth or the graft to the plough,
Not only sweet life for its kind, as the instincts allow,
That savour and shape may survive generations from now,
But life to its kin who can say, "I am stronger than thou,"
Fulfilling a lordlier law than the law of the bough.

I heard before dawn, with planets beginning to quail,
"Whoso hath life, let him give, that my purpose prevail:
Whoso hath none, let him take, that his strength may be hale.

Behold, I have reckoned the tally, I keep the full tale.
Whoso hath love, let him give, lest his spirit grow stale;
Whoso hath none, let him die; he shall wither and fail.
Behold I will plenish the loss at the turn of the scale.
He hath law to himself, who hath love; ye shall hope and not quail."

Then the sun arose, and my sunflowers here on the hill,
In free ceremonial turned to the East to fulfil
Their daily observance, receiving his peace and his will,
The lord of their light who alone bids the darkness be nil,
The lord of their love who alone bids the life in them thrill;
Undismayed and serene, they awaited him here on the hill.

Ah, the patience of earth! Look down at the dark pointed firs;
They are carved out of blackness; one pattern recurs and recurs.
They crowd all the gullies and hillsides, the gashes and spurs,
As silent as death. What an image! How nature avers
The goodness of calm with that taciturn beauty of hers!
As silent as sleep. Yet the life in them climbs and upstirs.
They too have received the great law, know that haste but defers
The perfection of time, the initiate gospeller firs.

So year after year, slow ring upon ring, they have grown,
Putting infinite long-loving care into leafage and cone,
By the old ancient craft of the earth they have pondered and known
In the dead of the hot summer noons, as still as a stone.
Not for them the gay fruit of the thorn, nor the high scarlet roan,
Nor the plots of the deep orchard-land where the apples are grown.

In winter the wind, all huddled and shuddering, came
To warm his old bones by the fires of sunset aflame
Behind trip black house of the firs. When the moose-birds grew tame
In the lumberer's camps in the woods, what marvellous fame
His talk and the ice of his touch would spread and proclaim,
Of the berg and the floe of the lands without nation or name,
Where the earth and the sky, night and noon, north and south are the same,
The white and awful Nirvana of cold whence he came!

Then April, some twilight picked out with a great yellow star,
Returning, like Hylas long lost and come back with his jar
Of sweet living water at last, having wandered so far,
Leads the heart out-of-doors, and the eye to the point of a spar,
At whose base in the half-melted snow the first Mayflowers are, —
 And there the first robin is pealing below the great star.

So soon, oversoon, the full summer. Within those dark boughs,
Deliberate and far, a faltering reed-note will rouse
The shy transports of earth, till the wood-creatures hear where they house,

And grow bold as the tremble-eared rabbits that nibble and mouse.
While up through the pasture-lot, startling the sheep as they browse,
Where kingbirds and warblers are piercing the heat's golden drowse,
Some girl, whom the sun has made tawny, the wind had to blowse,
Will come there to gentle her lover beneath those dark boughs.

Then out of the hush, when the grasses are frosty and old,
Will the chickadee's tiny alarm against winter be rolled;
And soon, when the ledges and ponds are bitten with cold,
The honk of the geese, that wander-cry stirring and bold,
Will sound through the night, where those hardy mariners hold
The uncharted course through the dark, as it is from of old.

Ah, the life of the woods, how they share and partake of it all,
These evergreens, silent as Indians, solemn and tall!
From the goldenwing's first far-heard awakening call,
The serene flute of the thrush in his high beech hall,
And the pipe of the frog, to the bannered approach of the fall,
And the sullen wind, when snow arrives on a squall,
Trooping in all night from the North with news would appal
Any outposts but these ; with a zest they partake of it all.

Lo, out of the hush they seem to mount and aspire!
From basement to tip they have builded, with heed to go higher,
One circlet of branches a year with their lift of green spire.
Nay, rather they seem to repose, having done with desire,

A SHEPHERD IN LESBOS

On her mouth she laid a warning finger,
And her slow calm enigmatic smile
Told me, ere she spoke, one-half the message;
Then I heard (my heart stood still the while),

"Mortal, wouldst thou know the maddening transport
No mere earth-born lover may attain,
Till some woodland deity hath loved him,
And her beauty mounted to his brain?

"Thenceforth he becomes, with her for mistress,
Master of the moods and minds of men,
Moulding as he will their deeds and daring,
All their follies open to his ken;

"Yet is he a wanderer forever,
Without respite seeking the unknown.

Wouldst thou leave the world for one who offers
But the beauty bounded by her zone?"

When I woke in golden morning dyeing
The dark valley and the purple hill,
Flushing at the doorway of the forest,
Flowered my mountain laurel, cool and still.

How I chose? Have ye not heard in Lesbos
Of a mad young shepherd by the shore,
Whose wild piping bids the traveller tarry
Some immortal sorrow to deplore?

On a morning by the river marges
Many a passer-by hath heard that strain,
Sweet and sad and strange and full of longing
As a bird-note through the purple rain.

In a maze the haunted music holds them
With its meaning past all guess or care;
With its magic note the lonely cadence
Swells and sinks and dies upon the air;

And they say, "It is the stricken shepherd
Whom the nymph's enchantment set astray,
And the spell of his bewildering vision
Holds him fast a lover from that day.

"His dark theme no mortal may interpret;
But forever when the wood-pipes blow,
Some remembered and mysterious echo
Calls us unresisting and we go."

DAPHNE

I know that face!
In some lone forest place,
When June brings back the laurel to the hills,
Where shade and sunlight lace,

Where all day long
The brown birds make their song
A music that seems never to have known
Dismay nor haste nor wrong

I once before

Have seen thee by the shore,
As if about to shed the flowery guise
And be thyself once more.

Dear, shy, soft face,
With just the elfin trace
That lends thy human beauty the last touch
Of wild, elusive grace!

Can it be true,
A god did once pursue
Thy gleaming beauty through the glimmering wood,
Drenched in the Dorian dew,

Too mad to stay
His hot and headstrong way,
Demented by the fragrance of thy flight,
Heedless of thy dismay?

But I to thee
More gently fond would be,
Nor less a lover woo thee with soft words
And woodland melody;

Take pipe and play
Each forest fear away;
Win thee to idle in the leafy shade
All the long Summer day;

Tell thee old tales
Of love, that still avails
More than all mighty things in this great world,
Still wonderworks nor fails;

Teach thee new lore,
How to love more and more,
And find the magical delirium
In joys unguessed before.

I would try over
And over to discover
Some wild, sweet, foolish, irresistible
New way to be thy lover

New, wondrous ways
To fill thy golden days,
Thy lovely pagan body with delight,
Thy loving heart with praise.

For I would learn,
Deep in the brookside fern,
The magic of the syrinx whispering low
With bubbly fall and turn;

Mock every note
Of the green woodbird's throat,
Till some wild strain, impassioned yet serene,
Should form and float

Far through the hills,
Where mellow sunlight fills
The world with joy, and from the purple vines
The brew of life distils.

Ah, then indeed
Thy heart should have no need
To tremble at a footfall in the brake,
And bid thy bright limbs speed.

But night would come,
And I should make thy home
In the deep pines, lit by a yellow star
Hung in the dark blue dome

A fragrant house
Of woven balsam boughs,
Where the great Cyprian mother should receive
Our warm unsullied vows.

THE LOST DRYAD

Where are you gone from the forest,
Leaving the mountain-side lonely
And all the beech woods deserted,
O my dear Daphne?

All the day long I go seeking
Trace of your flowerlike footprint.
Will not the dew on the meadow
Tell tale of Daphne?

Will not the sand on the sea-shore
Treasure that magical impress
For the disconsolate longing
Lover of Daphne?

Will not the moss and the fern-bed
Bearing the mould of her beauty,
Tell me where wandered and rested
Rose-golden Daphne?

All the night through I go hearkening
Every wild murmurous echo,
Hint of your laughter, the birdlike
Voice of my Daphne.

Why do the poplar leaves whisper
Things to themselves in the silence,
Though no wind visits the valley,
Daphne, my Daphne?

Listen! I hear their small voices,
An elfin multitude, mingle,
Lisping in silver-leaf language,
"Daphne, O Daphne!"

Listen! I hear the cold hill-brook
Plash down the clove on its pebbles,
And the ravine drenched in moonlight
Echoing, "Daphne!"

"Daphne," the rain says at nightfall;
"Daphne," the wind breathes at morning;
And a voice troubles the hot noon
Uttering "Daphne."

Ah, what impassioned remembrance,
In the dark pines in the starlight,
Touches the dream of your wood-thrush,
O my lost Daphne,

Dyeing his sleep like a bubble
Coloured for joy, and the note comes,
Golden, enchanted, eternal,
Calling for Daphne!

O Mother Earth, at how many
Thresholds of lone-dwelling mortals
Must I, a wayfarer, tarry,
Asking for Daphne?

How many times see their faces
Fade to incredulous wonder,

Hearing in some remote vale
The story of Daphne,

Ere I at last through the twilight
Hear the soft rapturous outcry,
And as of old there will greet me
Far-wandered Daphne?

THE DEAD FAUN

Who hath done this thing? What wonder is this that lies
On the green earth so still under purple skies,
Like a hyacinth shaft the careless mower has cut
And thought of no more?

Who hath wrought this pitiful wrong on the lovely earth?
What ruthless hand could ruin that harmless mirth?
O heart of things, what undoing is here, never now
To be mended more!

No more, O beautiful boy, shall thy fleet feet stray
Through the cool beech wood on the shadowy mountain way,
Nor halt by the well at noon, nor trample the flowers
On the forest floor.

Thy beautiful light-seeing gold-green eyes, so glad
When day came over the hill, so wondrous sad
When the burning sun went slowly under the sea,
Shall look no more.

Thy nimble fingers that plucked the fruit from the bough,
Or fondled the nymph's bright hair and filleted brow,
Or played the wild mellow pipe of thy father Pan,
Shall play no more.

Thy sensitive ears that knew all the speech of the wood,
Every call of the birds and the creatures, and understood
What the wind to the water said, what the river replied,
Shall hear no more.

Thy scarlet and lovely mouth which the dryads knew,
Dear whimsical ardent mouth that love spoke through,
For all the kisses of life that it took and gave,
Shall say no more.

Who hath trammelled those feet that never again shall rove?

Who hath bound these hands that never again shall move?
Who hath quenched the lamp in those eyes that never again
Shall be lighted more?

THE WORD AT ST. KAVIN'S

Once at St. Kavin's door
I rested. No sign more
Of discontent escaped me from that day.
For there I overheard
A Brother of the Word
Expound the grace of poverty, and say:

Thank God for poverty
That makes and keeps us free,
That lets us go our unobtrusive way,
Glad of the sun and rain,
Upright, serene, humane,
Contented with the fortune of a day.

Light-hearted as a bird,
I will obey the word
That bade the earth take form, the sea subside, —
That bids the wild wings go
Each year from line to snow,
When Spring unfurls her old green flag for guide, —

That bids the fleeting hosts
Along the shelving coasts
Once more adventure far by sound and stream,
Bids everything alive
Awaken and revive,
Resume the unperished glory and the dream.

I too, with fear put by,
Confront my destiny,
With not a wish but to arise and go,
Where beauty still may lead
From creed to larger creed,
Thanking my Maker that he made me so.

For I would shun no task
That kindliness may ask,
Nor flinch at any duty to my kind;
Praying but to be freed
From ignorance and greed,

Grey fear and dull despondency of mind.

So I would readjust
The logic of the dust,
The servile hope that puts its trust in things.
Ephemera of earth,
Of more than fleeting worth,
Are we, endowed with rapture as with wings.

(Type of the soul of man,
The slight yet stable plan!
Those creatures perishable as the dew,
How buoyantly they ride
The vast and perilous tide.
Free as the air their courses to pursue!)

And I would keep my soul
Joyous and sane and whole,
Unshamed by falsehood and unvexed by strife,
Unalien in that clear
And radiant atmosphere
That still surrounds us with a larger life,

When we have laid aside
Our truculence and pride,
Craven self-seeking, turbulent self-will,
Resolved this very day
No longer to obey
The tyrant Mammon who begods us still.

All selfish gain at best
Brings but profound unrest
And inward loss, despite our loud professions.
Think therefore what it is,
What surety of bliss,
To be absolved from burdensome possessions!

Shall God, who doth provide
The majesty and pride
And beauty of this earth so lavishly,
Deny them to the poor
And lowly and obscure?
Nay, they are .given to all justly and free.

And if I share my crust,
As common manhood must,
With one whose need is greater than my own,
Shall I not also give

His soul, that it may live,
Of the abundant pleasures I have known?

And so, if I have wrought,
Amassed or conceived aught
Of beauty or intelligence or power,
It is not mine to hoard;
It stands there to afford
Its generous service simply as a flower.

How soon, my friends, how soon
We should obtain the boon
Of shining peace for which the toiler delves,
If only we would give
Our spirit room to live, —
Be, here and now, our brave untarnished selves

If only we would dare
Espouse the good and fair
Our soul, unbound by custom, still perceives;
And without compromise
Or favour in men's eyes
Live by the truth each one of us believes!

Bow not to vested wrong
That we have served too long,
Pawning our birthright for a tinsel star!
Shall the soul take upon her
Time-service and mouth-honour?
Behold the fir-trees, how unswerved they are!

Native to sun and storm,
They cringe not nor conform,
Save to the gentle law their sound heart knows;
Each day enough for them
To rise, cone, branch, and stem,
A leaf-breadth higher in their tall repose.

Ah, what a travesty
Of man's ascent, were I
To bear myself less royally than they,
After the ages spent
In spirit's betterment,
Through rounds of aspiration and decay!

For surely I have grown
Within a cleft of stone,
With spray of mountain torrents in my face.

Slow soaring ring by ring
On moveless tiled wing,
I have seen earth below me sink through space.

I too in polar night
Have hungered, gaunt and white,
Alone amid the awful silences;
And fled on gaudy fin,
When the blue tides came in,
Through coral gardens under tropic seas.

And wheresoe'er I strove,
The greater law was love,
A faith too fine to falter or mistrust;
There was no wanton greed,
Depravity of breed,
Malice nor cant nor enmity unjust.

Nay, not till I was man,
Learned I to scheme and plan
The blackest depredation on my kind,
Converting to my gain
My fellow's need and pain,
In chartered pillage ruthless and refined.

Therefore, my friends, I say,
Back to the fair sweet way
Our mother Nature taught us long ago,
The large primeval mood,
Leisure and amplitude,
The dignity of patience strong and slow.

Let us go in once more,
By some blue mountain door,
And hold communion with the forest leaves,
Where long ago we trod
The Ghost House of the God,
Through orange dawns and amethystine eves.

There bright-robed choristers
Make music in the firs,
Rejoicing in their service all day long;
And there the whole night through,
Along the dark still blue,
What glorying hosts with starry tapers throng!

There in some deep ravine
Whose walls are living green,

A sanctuary spacious, cool, and dim,
At earth-refreshing morn,
The pure white clouds are born,
The incense of the ground sent up to Him.

No slighted task is there,
But equal craft and care
And love in irresistible accord,
The test and sign of art,
Bestowed through every part;
No thought of recognition or reward.

In that diviner air
We shall grow wise and fair,
Not frayed by hurry nor distraught by noise, -
Learn once again to be
Noble, courageous, free,
Regain our primal ecstasy and poise.

Calm in the deep control
Of firmamental soul,
Let us abide unfretful and secure,
Knowledge and reason bent
To further soul's intent,
Her veiled dim purposes remote yet sure.

For soul has led us now,
Science unravels how,
Through cell and tissue up from dust to man;
And will lead by and by,
No logic tells us why,
To fill her purport in the ampler plan.

Ah, trust the soul, my friends,
To seek her own great ends
Revealed not in the fashion of the hour!
For 'she outlives intact
The insufficient act,
Herself the source and channel of all power.

The soul survives, unmarred,
The mind care-worn and scarred,
That still is anxious over little things,
To come unto her own,
Through benefits unknown
And the green beauty of a thousand springs.

From infinite resource

She holds her gleaming course
Through toil, distraction, hindrance, and dismay,
Till some high destiny,
Accomplished by and by,
Reveals the splendid hope that was her stay.

Therefore should every hour
Replenish her with power
Of joy and love and freedom and fresh truth,
That we even in age
May share her heritage
Of ancient wisdom with the heart of youth.

Lore of the worldly wise
Is folly in her eyes.
All-energy, all-knowledge, and all-love,
Aware of deeps below
This pageant that we know,
Hers is the very faith accounted of

By Him who rose and bade
His friends be not afraid,
When peril rocked their fishing-boat at sea, —
Who bade the sick not fear,
The sad be of good cheer,
And in the hour they were made whole and free.

The sceptic sees but part
Of Nature's mighty heart.
A wide berth would I give that dangerous shoal
Steer for the open sea,
No sight of land, but free.
Trusting my senses, shall I doubt my soul?

Let me each day anew
My outward voyage pursue
For the Far Islands and the Apple Lands.
Till through the breaking gloom
Some evening they shall loom,
With one pale star above the lilac sands.

Ah, that day I shall know
How the shy wood-flowers grow
In the deep forest, turning to the light;
Untrammelled impulse still
With glad obedient will
The only guide out of ancestral night.

Oh, I shall comprehend
Truth at my journey's end,
What being is, and what I strive to be, —
What soul in beauty's guise
Eludes our wistful eyes,
Yet surely is akin to you and me.

Therefore, towards that supreme
Knowledge, that unveiled dream,
That promise of our life from day to day,
The grace of joyousness
Abide with us to bless
And help us forth along the Perfect Way!

The voice of the good priest
In benediction ceased;
The congregation like a murmur rose;
And when I set my pack
Once more upon my back,
'Twas light as any thistle-down that blows.

CHRISTMAS EVE AT ST. KAVIN'S

To the assembled folk
At great St. Kavin's spoke
Young Brother Amiel on Christmas eve;
I give you joy, my friends,
That as the round year ends,
We meet once more for gladness by God's leave.

On other festal days
For penitence or praise
Or prayer we meet, or fulness of thanksgiving;
To-night we calendar
The rising of that star'
Which lit the old world with new joy of living.

Ah, we disparage still
The Tidings of Good Will,
Discrediting Love's gospel now as then!
And with the verbal creed
That God is love indeed,
Who dares make Love his god before all men:

Shall we not, therefore, friends,
Resolve to make amends

To that glad inspiration of the heart;
To grudge not, to cast out
Selfishness, malice, doubt,
Anger and fear; and for the better part,

To love so much, so well,
The spirit cannot tell
The range and sweep of her own boundary!
There is no period
Between the soul and God;
Love is the tide, God the eternal sea.

Of old, men walked by fear;
And if their God seemed near,
It was the Avenger unto whom they bowed, —
A wraith of their own woes,
Vain, cruel, and morose,
With anger and vindictiveness endowed.

Of old, men walked by hate;
The ruthless were the great;
Their crumbling kingdoms stayed by might alone.
Men saw vast empires die,
Nor guessed the reason why, —
The simple law of life as yet unknown

As love. Then came our Lord,
Proclaiming the accord
Of soul and nature in love's rule and sway,
The lantern that he set
To light us, shining yet
Along the Perfect Path wherein we stray.

To-day we walk by love;
To strive is not enough,
Save against greed and ignorance and might.
We apprehend peace comes
Not with the roll of drums,
But in the still processions of the night.

And we perceive, not awe
But love is the great law
That binds the world together safe and whole.
The splendid planets run
Their courses in the sun;
Love is the gravitation of the soul.

In the profound unknown,

Illumined, fair, and lone,
Each star is set to shimmer in its place.
In the profound divine
Each soul is set to shine,
And its unique appointed orbit trace.

There is no near nor far,
Where glorious Algebar
Swings round his mighty circuit through the night,
Yet where without a sound
The winged seed comes to ground,
And the red leaf seems hardly to alight.

One force, one lore, one need
For satellite and seed,
In the serene benignity for all.
Letting her time-glass run
With star-dust, sun by sun,
In Nature's thought there is no great nor small.

There is no far nor near
Within the spirit's sphere.
The summer sunset's scarlet-yellow wings
Are tinged with the same dye
That paints the tulip's ply.
And what is colour but the soul of things?

(The earth was without form;
God moulded it with storm,
Ice, flood, and tempest, gleaming tint and hue;
Lest it should come to ill
For lack of spirit still,
He gave it colour, — let the love shine through.)

My joy of yesterday
Is just as far away
As the first rapture of my man's estate.
A lifetime or an hour
Has all there is of power.
In Nature's love there is no small nor great.

Of old, men said, "Sin not;
By every line and jot
Ye shall abide; man's heart is false and vile."
Christ said, " By Love alone
In man's heart is God known;
Obey the word no falsehood can defile."

The wise physician there
Of our distress had care,
And laid his finger on the pulse of time.
And there to eyes unsealed
Earth's secret lay revealed,
The truth that knows not any age nor clime.

The heart of the ancient wood
Was a grim solitude,
The sanction of a worship no less grim;
Man's ignorance and fear
Peopled the natural year
With forces evil and malign to him.

He saw the wild, rough way
Of cosmic powers at play;
He did not see the love that lay below.
Jehovah, Mars, and Thor,
These were the gods of war
He made in his own likeness long ago.

Then came the Word, and said,
"See how the world is made, —
With how much loving kindness, ceaseless care.
Not Wrath, but Love, call then
The Lord of beasts and men,
Whose hand sustains the sparrows in the air."

And since that day we prove
Only how great is love,
Nor to this hour its greatness half believe.
For to what other power
Will life give equal dower,
Or chaos grant one moment of reprieve!

Look down the ages' line,
Where slowly the divine
Evinces energy, puts forth control;
See mighty love alone
Transmuting stock and stone,
Infusing being, helping sense and soul.

And what is energy,
In-working, which bids be
The starry pageant and the life of earth?
What is the genesis
Of every joy and bliss,
Each action dared, each beauty brought to birth?

What hangs the sun on high?
What swells the growing rye?
What bids the loons cry on the Northern lake?
What stirs in swamp and swale,
When April winds prevail,
And all the dwellers of the ground awake?

What lurks in the dry seed,
But waiting to be freed,
Asleep and patient for a hundred years?
Till of earth, rain, and sun,
A miracle is done.
Some magic calls the sleeper and he hears,—

Arouses, puts forth blade
And leaf and bud, arrayed
Some morning in that garb of rosy snow,
The same fair matchless flower
As shed its petal-shower
Through old Iberean gardens long ago.

What is it that endures,
Survives, persists, immures
Life's very self, preserving type and plan? —
Yet learns the scope of change,
As the long cycles range, —
Looks through the eyes of bluebird, wolf, and man?

What lurks in the deep gaze
Of the old wolf? Amaze,
Hope, recognition, gladness, anger, fear.
But deeper than all these
Love muses, yearns, and sees,
And is the self that does not change nor veer,

Not love of self alone,
Struggle for lair and bone,
But self-denying love of mate and young,
Love that is kind and wise,
Knows trust and sacrifice,
And croons the old dark universal tongue.

In Nature you behold
But strivings manifold,
Battle and conflict, tribe warring against tribe?
Look deeper, and see all
That death cannot appal,

Failure intimidate, nor fortune bribe.

Our brothers of the air
Who come with June must dare,
Be bold and strong, have knowledge, lust, and choice;
Yet think, when glad hosts throng
The summer woods with song,
Love gave them beauty and love lends them voice.

Love surely in some form
Bade them brave night and storm,
Was the dark binnacle that held them true,
Those tiny mariners
No unknown voyage deters,
When the old migrant longing stirs anew.

And who has understood
Our brothers of the wood,
Save he who put off guile and every guise
Of violence, made truce
With panther, bear, and moose,
As beings like ourselves whom love makes wise?

For they, too, do love's will,
Our lesser clansmen still;
The House of Many Mansions holds us all;
Courageous, glad, and hale,
They go forth on the trail,
Hearing the message, hearkening to the call.

Oh, not fortuitous chance
Alone, nor circumstance,
Begot the creatures after their own kind;
But always loving will
Was present to fulfil
The primal purpose groping up to mind.

Adversity but bade
New puissance spring to aid,
New powers develop, new aptness come in play;
Yet never function wrought
Capacity from nought,
Gave skill and mastery to the shapes of clay;

For always while new need
Evoked new thought through deed.
Old self was there to ponder, choose, and strive.
Fortune might mould, evolve,

But impulse must resolve,
Equipped at length to know, rejoice, and thrive.

And evermore must Love
Hearten, foresee, approve,
And look upon the work and find it good;
Else would all effort fail,
The very stars avail
Less than a swarm of fireflies in a wood.

Take love out of the world
One day, and we are hurled
Back into night, to perish in the void.
Love is the very girth
And cincture of this earth,
No stitch to be unloosed, no link destroyed.

However wild and long
The battle of the strong,
Stronger and longer are the hours of peace,
When gladness has its way
Under the fair blue day,
And life aspires, takes thought, bids good increase.

So dawns the awaited hour
When the great cosmic power
Of love was first declared by Christ; so too
To-day we keep in mind
His name who taught mankind
That open secret old, yet ever new, —

Commemorate his birth
Who loved the kindly earth,
Was gentle, strong, compassionate, humane,
And tolerant and wise
And glad, — the very guise
And height of manhood not to lose again.

Shall we not then forego
Lavish perfunctory show,
The burdensome display, the empty gift,
That we may have to give
To every soul alive
Of love's illumination, cheer, and lift?

See rich and poor be fed!
Break up thy soul for bread,
Be loaves and fishes to the hungry heart,

That a great multitude,
Receiving of thy good,
May bless the God within thee and depart!

You workman, love your work
Or leave it. Let no irk
Unsteady the laborious hand, that still
Must give the spirit play
To follow her own way
To beauty, through devotion, care, and skill.

How otherwise find vent
For soul's imperious bent,
Than thro' these hands for wonder-working made,
When Love the sure and bold
Guides to the unforetold?
Blessed the craftsman who is unafraid!

Give Beauty her sweet will,
Make love your mistress still,
You lovers, nor delay! God's time be yours.
Make low-born jealousy
And doubt ashamed to be,
And cast old envious gossip out-of-doors.

Believe the truth of love,
Enact the beauty of love,
Praise and adore the goodliness of love.
For we are wise by love,
And strong and fair through love,
No less than sainted and inspired with love.

Remember the new word
The Syrian twilight heard,
That marvellous discourse which John records,
The one last great command
The Master left his band,
"Love one another!" And our time affords

What greater scope than just
To execute that trust?
Love greatly; love; love is life's best employ.
Neighbour, sweetheart, or friend,
Love wholly, to love's end;
So is the round world richer for your joy.

Love only, one or all!
Measure no great and small!

Love is a seed, life-bearing, undecayed;
And that immortal germ
Past bounds of zone and term
Will grow and cover the whole world with shade.

Sow love, it cannot fail;
Adversity's sharp hail
May cut all else to ground; fair love survives.
The black frost of despair
And slander's bitter air,
Love will outlast them by a thousand lives.

Be body, mind and soul,
Subject to love's control,
Each loving to the limit of love's power;
And all as one, not three,
So is man's trinity
Enhanced and freed and gladdened hour by hour.

Beauty from youth to age,
The body's heritage,
Love will not forfeit by neglect nor shame;
And knowledge, dearly bought,
Love will account as nought,
Unless it serve soul's need and body's claim.

Let soul desire, mind ask,
And body crave; our task
Be to fulfil each want in love's own way.
So shall the good and true
Partake of beauty too,
And life be helped and greatened day by day.

Spend love, and save it not;
In act, in wish, in thought,
Spend love upon this lifetime without stint.
Let not the heart grow dry,
As the good hours go by;
Love now, see earth take on the glory tint.

Open the door to-night
Within your heart, and light
The lantern of love there to shine afar.
On a tumultuous sea
Some straining craft, maybe,
With bearings lost, shall sight love's silver star.

How many Canadians—how many even among the few who seek to keep themselves informed of the best in contemporary literature, who are ever on the alert for the new voices—realise, or even suspect, that this Northern land of theirs has produced a poet of whom it may be affirmed with confidence and assurance that he is of the great succession of English poets? Yet such—strange and unbelievable though it may seem—is in very truth the case, that poet being (to give him his full name) William Bliss Carman. Canada has full right to be proud of her poets, a small body though they are; but not only does Mr. Carman stand high and clear above them all—his place (and time cannot but confirm and justify the assertion) is among those men whose poetry is the shining glory of that great English literature which is our common heritage.

If any should ask why, if what has been just said is so, there has been—as must be admitted—no general recognition of the fact in the poet's home land, I would answer that there are various and plausible, if not good, reasons for it.

First of all, the poet, as thousands more of our young men of ambition and confidence have done, went early to the United States, and until recently, except for rare and brief visits to his old home down by the sea, has never returned to Canada—though for all that, I am able to state, on his own authority, he is still a Canadian citizen. Then all his books have had their original publication in the United States, and while a few of them have subsequently carried the imprints of Canadian publishers, none of these can be said ever to have made any special effort to push their sale. Another reason for the fact above mentioned is that Mr. Carman has always scorned to advertise himself, while his work has never been the subject of the log-rolling and booming which the work of many another poet has had—to his ultimate loss. A further reason is that he follows a rule of his own in preparing his books for publication. Most poets publish a volume of their work as soon as, through their industry and perseverance, they have material enough on hand to make publication desirable in their eyes. Not so with Mr. Carman, however, his rule being not to publish until he has done sufficient work of a certain general character or key to make a volume. As a result, you cannot fully know or estimate his work by one book, or two books, or even half a dozen; you must possess or be familiar with every one of the score and more volumes which contain his output of poetry before you can realise how great and how many-sided is his genius.

It is a common remark on the part of those who respond readily to the vigorous work of Kipling, or Masefield, even our own Service, that Bliss Carman's poetry has no relation to or concern with ordinary, everyday life. One would suppose that most persons who cared for poetry at all turned to it as a relief from or counter to the burdens and vexations of the daily round; but in any event, the remark referred to seems to me to indicate either the most casual acquaintance with Mr. Carman's work, or a complete misunderstanding and misapprehension of the meaning of it. I grant that you will find little or nothing in it all to remind you of the grim realities and vexing social problems of this modern existence of ours; but to say or to suggest that these things do not exist for Mr. Carman is to say or to suggest something which is the reverse of true. The truth is, he is aware of them as only one with the sensitive organism of a poet can be; but he does not feel that he has a call or mission to remedy them, and still less to sing of them. He therefore leaves the immediate problems of the day to those who choose, or are led, to occupy themselves therewith, and turns resolutely away to dwell upon those things which for him possess infinitely greater importance.

"What are they?" one who knows Mr. Carman only as, say, a lyrist of spring or as a singer of the delights of vagabondia probably will ask in some wonder. Well, the things which concern him above all, I would answer, are first, and naturally, the beauty and wonder of this world of ours, and next the mystery of the earthly pilgrimage of the human soul out of eternity and back into it again.

The poems in the present volume—which, by the way, can boast the high honor of being the very first regular Canadian edition of his work—will be evidence ample and conclusive to every reader, I am sure, of the place which

The perennial enchanted
Lovely world and all its lore

occupy in the heart and soul of Bliss Carman, as well as of the magical power with which he is able to convey the deep and unfailing satisfaction and delight which they possess for him. They, however, represent his latest period (he has had three well-defined periods), comprising selections from three of his last published volumes: The Rough Rider, Echoes from Vagabondia, and April Airs, together with a number of new poems, and do not show, except here and there and by hints and flashes, how great is his preoccupation with the problem of man's existence—

—the hidden import
Of man's eternal plight.

This is manifest most in certain of his earlier books, for in these he turns and returns to the greatest of all the problems of man almost constantly, probing, with consummate and almost unrivalled use of the art of expression, for the secret which surely, he clearly feels, lies hidden somewhere, to be discovered if one could but pierce deeply enough. Pick up Behind the Arras, and as you turn over page after page you cannot but observe how incessantly the poet's mind—like the minds of his two great masters, Browning and Whitman—works at this problem. In "Behind the Arras," the title poem; "In the Wings," "The Crimson House," "The Lodger," "Beyond the Gamut," "The Juggler"—yes, in every poem in the book—he takes up and handles the strange thing we know as, or call, life, turning it now this way, now that, in an effort to find out its meaning and purpose. He comes but little nearer success in this than do most of the rest of men, of course; but the magical and ever-fresh beauty of his expression, the haunting melody of his lines, the variety of his images and figures and the depth and range of his thought, put his searchings and ponderings in a class by themselves.

Lengthy quotation from Mr. Carman's books is not permitted here, and I must guide myself accordingly, though with reluctance, because I believe that in a study such as this the subject should be allowed to speak for himself as much as possible. In "Behind the Arras" the poet describes the passage from life to death as

A cadence dying down unto its source
In music's course,

and goes on to speak of death as

—the broken rhythm of thought and man,
The sweep and span
Of memory and hope

About the orbit where they still must grope
For wider scope,

To be through thousand springs restored, renewed,
With love imbrued,
With increments of will
Made strong, perceiving unattainment still
From each new skill.

Now follow some verses from "Behind the Gamut," to my mind the poet's greatest single achievement;

As fine sand spread on a disc of silver,
At some chord which bids the motes combine,
Heeding the hidden and reverberant impulse,
Shifts and dances into curve and line,

The round earth, too, haply, like a dust-mote,
Was set whirling her assigned sure way,
Round this little orb of her ecliptic
To some harmony she must obey.

And what of man?

Linked to all his half-accomplished fellows,
Through unfrontiered provinces to range—
Man is but the morning dream of nature,
Roused to some wild cadence weird and strange.

Here, now, are some verses from "Pulvis et Umbra," which is to be found in Mr. Carman's first book, Low Tide on Grand Pré, and in which the poet addresses a moth which a storm has blown into his window:

For man walks the world with mourning
Down to death and leaves no trace,
With the dust upon his forehead,
And the shadow on his face.

Pillared dust and fleeing shadow
As the roadside wind goes by,
And the fourscore years that vanish
In the twinkling of an eye.

"Pillared dust and fleeing shadow." Where in all our English literature will one find the life history of man summed up more briefly and, at the same time, more beautifully, than in that wonderful line? Now follows a companion verse to those just quoted, taken from "Lord of My Heart's Elation," which stands in the forefront of From the Green Book of the Bards. It may be remarked here that while the poet recurs again and again to some favorite thought or idea, it is never in the same words. His expression is always new and fresh, showing how deep and true is his inspiration. Again it is man who is pictured:

A fleet and shadowy column
Of dust and mountain rain,
To walk the earth a moment
And be dissolved again.

But while Mr. Carman's speculations upon life's meaning and the mystery of the future cannot but appeal to the thoughtful-minded, it is as an interpreter of nature that he makes his widest appeal. Bliss Carman, I must say here, and emphatically, is no mere landscape-painter; he never, or scarcely ever, paints a picture of nature for its own sake. He goes beyond the outward aspect of things and interprets or translates for us with less keen senses as only a poet whose feeling for nature is of the deepest and profoundest, who has gone to her whole-heartedly and been taken close to her warm bosom, can do. Is this not evident from these verses from "The Great Return"—originally called "The Pagan's Prayer," and for some inscrutable reason to be found only in the limited Collected Poems, issued in two stately volumes in 1905.

When I have lifted up my heart to thee,
Thou hast ever hearkened and drawn near,
And bowed thy shining face close over me,
Till I could hear thee as the hill-flowers hear.

When I have cried to thee in lonely need,
Being but a child of thine bereft and wrung,
Then all the rivers in the hills gave heed;
And the great hill-winds in thy holy tongue—

That ancient incommunicable speech—
The April stars and autumn sunsets know—
Soothed me and calmed with solace beyond reach
Of human ken, mysterious and low.

Who can read or listen to those moving lines without feeling that Mr. Carman is in very truth a poet of nature—nay, Nature's own poet? But how could he be other when, in "The Breath of the Reed" (From the Green Book of the Bards), he makes the appeal?

Make me thy priest, O Mother,
And prophet of thy mood,
With all the forest wonder
Enraptured and imbued.

As becomes such a poet, and particularly a poet whose birth-month is April, Mr. Carman sings much of the early spring. Again and again he takes up his woodland pipe, and lo! Pan himself and all his train troop joyously before us. Yet the singer's notes for all his singing never become wearied or strident; his airs are ever new and fresh; his latest songs are no less spontaneous and winning than were his first, written how many years ago, while at the same time they have gained in beauty and melody. What heart will not stir to the vibrant music of his immortal "Spring Song," which was originally published in the first Songs from Vagabondia, and the opening verses of which follow?

Make me over, mother April,

When the sap begins to stir!
When thy flowery hand delivers
All the mountain-prisoned rivers,
And thy great heart beats and quivers
To revive the days that were,
Make me over, mother April,
When the sap begins to stir!

Take my dust and all my dreaming,
Count my heart-beats one by one,
Send them where the winters perish;
Then some golden noon recherish
And restore them in the sun,
Flower and scent and dust and dreaming,
With their heart-beats every one!

That poem is sufficient in itself to prove that Bliss Carman has full right and title to be called Spring's own lyrist, though it may be remarked here that not all his spring poems are so unfeignedly joyous. Many of them indeed, have a touch, or more than a touch, of wistfulness, for the poet knows well that sorrow lurks under all joy, deep and well hidden though it may be.

Mr. Carman sings equally finely, though perhaps not so frequently, of summer and the other seasons; but as he has other claims upon our attention, I shall forbear to labor the fact, particularly as the following collection demonstrates it sufficiently. One of those other claims is as a writer of sea poetry. Few poets, it may be said, have pictured the majesty and the mystery, the beauty and the terror of the sea, better than he. His Ballads of Lost Haven is a veritable treasure-house for those whose spirits find kinship in wide expanses of moving waters. One of the best known poems in this volume is "The Gravedigger," which opens thus:

Oh, the shambling sea is a sexton old,
And well his work is done.
With an equal grave for lord and knave,
He buries them every one.

Then hoy and rip, with a rolling hip,
He makes for the nearest shore;
And God, who sent him a thousand ship,
Will send him a thousand more;
But some he'll save for a bleaching grave,
And shoulder them in to shore—
Shoulder them in, shoulder them in,
Shoulder them in to shore.

In "The City of the Sea" (Last Songs from Vagabondia) Mr. Carman speaks of the seabells sounding

The eternal cadence of sea sorrow
For Man's lot and immemorial wrong—
The lost strains that haunt the human dwelling

With the ghost of song.

Elsewhere he speaks of

The great sea, mystic and musical.

And here from another poem is a striking picture:

... the old sea
Seems to whimper and deplore
Mourning like a childless crone
With her sorrow left alone—
The eternal human cry
To the heedless passer-by.

I have said above that Mr. Carman has had three distinct periods, and intimated that the poems in the following collection are of his third period. The first period may be said to be represented by the Low Tide and Behind the Arras volumes, while the second is displayed in the three volumes of Songs from Vagabondia, which he published in association with his friend Richard Hovey. Bliss Carman was from the first too original and individual a poet to be directly influenced by anyone else; but there can be no doubt that his friendship with Hovey helped to turn him from over-preoccupation with mysteries which, for all their greatness, are not for man to solve, to an intenser realisation of the beauty and loveliness of the world about him and of the joys of human fellowship. The result is seen in such poems as "Spring Song," quoted in part above, and his perhaps equally well-known "The Joys of the Road," which appeared in the same volume with that poem, and a few verses from which follow:

Now the joys of the road are chiefly these:
A crimson touch on the hardwood trees;

A vagrant's morning wide and blue,
In early fall, when the wind walks, too;

A shadowy highway cool and brown,
Alluring up and enticing down

From rippled waters and dappled swamp,
From purple glory to scarlet pomp;

The outward eye, the quiet will,
And the striding heart from hill to hill.

Some of the finest of arman's work is contained in his elegiac or memorial poems, in which he commemorates Keats, Shelley, William Blake, Lincoln, Stevenson, and other men for whom he has a kindred feeling, and also friends whom he has loved and lost. Listen to these moving lines from "Non Omnis Moriar," written in memory of Gleeson White, and to be found in Last Songs from Vagabondia:

There is a part of me that knows,
Beneath incertitude and fear,

I shall not perish when I pass
Beyond mortality's frontier;

But greatly having joyed and grieved,
Greatly content, shall hear the sigh
Of the strange wind across the lone
Bright lands of taciturnity.

In patience therefore I await
My friend's unchanged benign regard,—
Some April when I too shall be
Spilt water from a broken shard.

In "The White Gull," written for the centenary of the birth of Shelley in 1892, and included in By the Aurelian Wall, he thus apostrophizes that clear and shining spirit:

O captain of the rebel host,
Lead forth and far!
Thy toiling troopers of the night
Press on the unavailing fight;
The sombre field is not yet lost,
With thee for star.

Thy lips have set the hail and haste
Of clarions free
To bugle down the wintry verge
Of time forever, where the surge
Thunders and trembles on a waste
And open sea.

In "A Seamark," a threnody for Robert Louis Stevenson, which appears in the same volume, the poet hails "R.L.S." (of whose tribe he may be said to be truly one) as

The master of the roving kind,

and goes on:

O all you hearts about the world
In whom the truant gypsy blood,
Under the frost of this pale time,
Sleeps like the daring sap and flood
That dreams of April and reprieve!
You whom the haunted vision drives,
Incredulous of home and ease.
Perfection's lovers all your lives!

You whom the wander-spirit loves
To lead by some forgotten clue

Forever vanishing beyond
Horizon brinks forever new;
Our restless loved adventurer,
On secret orders come to him,
Has slipped his cable, cleared the reef,
And melted on the white sea-rim.

"Perfection's lovers all your lives." Of these, it may be said without qualification, is Bliss Carman himself.

No summary of Mr. Carman's work, however cursory, would be worthy of the name if it omitted mention of his ventures in the realm of Greek myth. From the Book of Myths is made up of work of that sort, every poem in it being full of the beauty of phrase and melody of which Mr. Carman alone has the secret. The finest poems in the book, barring the opening one, "Overlord," are "Daphne," "The Dead Faun," "Hylas," and "At Phædra's Tomb," but I can do no more here than name them, for extracts would fail to reveal their full beauty. And beauty, after all is said, is the first and last thing with Mr. Carman. As he says himself somewhere:

The joy of the hand that hews for beauty
Is the dearest solace under the sun.

And again

The eternal slaves of beauty
Are the masters of the world.

A slave—a happy, willing slave—to beauty is the poet himself, and the world can never repay him for the message of beauty which he has brought it.

Kindred to From the Book of Myths, but much more important, is Sappho: One Hundred Lyrics, one of the most successful of the numerous attempts which have been made to recapture the poems by that high priestess of song which remain to us only in fragments. Mr. Carman, as Charles G. D. Roberts points out in an introduction to the volume, has made no attempt here at translation or paraphrasing; his venture has been "the most perilous and most alluring in the whole field of poetry"—that of imaginative and, at the same time, interpretive construction. Brief quotation again would fail to convey an adequate idea of the exquisiteness of the work, and all I can do, therefore, is to urge all lovers of real poetry to possess themselves of Sappho: One Hundred Lyrics, for it is literally a storehouse of lyric beauty.

I must not fail here to speak of From the Book of Valentines, which contains some lovely things, notably "At the Great Release." This is not only one of the finest of all Mr. Carman's poems, but it is also one of the finest poems of our time. It is a love poem, and no one possessing any real feeling for poetry can read it without experiencing that strange thrill of the spirit which only the highest form of poetry can communicate. "Morning and Evening," "In an Iris Meadow," and "A letter from Lesbos" must be also mentioned. In the last named poem, Sappho is represented as writing to Gorgo, and expresses herself in these moving words:

If the high gods in that triumphant time
Have calendared no day for thee to come

Light-hearted to this doorway as of old,
Unmoved I shall behold their pomps go by—
The painted seasons in their pageantry,
The silvery progressions of the moon,
And all their infinite ardors unsubdued,
Pass with the wind replenishing the earth

Incredulous forever I must live
And, once thy lover, without joy behold,
The gradual uncounted years go by,
Sharing the bitterness of all things made.

Mention must be now made of Songs of the Sea Children, which can be described only as a collection of the sweetest and tenderest love lyrics written in our time—

—the lyric songs
The earthborn children sing,
When wild-wood laughter throngs
The shy bird-throats of spring;
When there's not a joy of the heart
But flies like a flag unfurled,
And the swelling buds bring back
The April of the world.

So perfect and complete are these lyrics that it would be almost sacrilege to quote any of them unless entire. Listen however, to these verses:

The day is lost without thee,
The night has not a star.
Thy going is an empty room
Whose door is left ajar.

Depart: it is the footfall
Of twilight on the hills.
Return: and every rood of ground
Breaks into daffodils.

There are those who will have it that Bliss Carman has been away from Canada so long that he has ceased to be, in a real sense, a Canadian. Such assume rather than know, for a very little study of his work would show them that it is shot through and through with the poet's feeling for the land of his birth. Memories of his childhood and youthful years down by the sea are still fresh in Mr. Carman's mind, and inspire him again and again in his writing. "A Remembrance," at the beginning of the present collection, may be pointed to as a striking instance of this, but proof positive is the volume, Songs from a Northern Garden, for it could have been written only by a Canadian, born and bred, one whose heart and soul thrill to the thought of Canada. I would single out from this volume for special mention as being "Canadian" in the fullest sense "In a Grand Pré Garden," "The Keeper's Silence," "At Home and Abroad," "Killoleet," and "Above the Gaspereau," but have no space to quote from them.

But Mr. Carman is not only a Canadian, he is also a Briton; and evidence of this is his Ode on the Coronation, written on the occasion of the crowning of King Edward VII in 1902. This poem—the very existence of which is hardly known among us—ought to be put in the hands of every child and youth who speaks the English tongue, for no other, I dare maintain—nothing by Kipling, or Newbolt, or any other of our so-called "Imperial singers"—expresses more truly and more movingly the deep feeling of love and reverence which the very thought of England evokes in every son of hers, even though it may never have been his to see her white cliffs rise or to tread her storied ground:

O England, little mother by the sleepless Northern tide,
Having bred so many nations to devotion, trust, and pride,
Very tenderly we turn
With welling hearts that yearn
Still to love you and defend you,—let the sons of men discern
Wherein your right and title, might and majesty, reside.

In concluding this, I greatly fear, lamentably inadequate study, I come to the collection which follows, and which, as intimated above, represents the work of Mr. Carman's latest period. I must say at once that, while I yield to no one in admiration for Low Tide and the other books of that period, or for the work of the second period, as represented by the Songs from Vagabondia volumes, I have no hesitation in declaring that I regard the poet's work of the past few years with even higher admiration. It may not possess the force and vigor of the work which preceded it; but anything seemingly missing in that respect is more than made up for me by increased beauty and clarity of expression. The mysticism—verging, or more than verging, at times on symbolism—which marked his earlier poems, and which hung, as it were, as a veil between them and the reader, has gone, and the poet's thought or theme now lies clearly before us as in a mirror. What—to take a verse from the following pages at random—could be more pellucid, more crystal clear in expression—what indeed, could come closer to that achieving of the impossible at which every real poet must aim—than this from "In Gold Lacquer".

Gold are the great trees overhead,
And gold the leaf-strewn grass,
As though a cloth of gold were spread
To let a seraph pass.
And where the pageant should go by,
Meadow and wood and stream,
The world is all of lacquered gold,
Expectant as a dream.

The poet, happily, has fully recovered from the serious illness which laid him low some two years ago, and which for a time caused his friends and admirers the gravest concern, and so we may look forward hopefully to seeing further volumes of verse come from the press to make certain his name and fame. But if, for any reason, this should not be—which the gods forfend!—Later Poems, I dare affirm, must and will be regarded as the fine flower and crowning achievement of the genius and art of Bliss Carman.

R. H. HATHAWAY.
Toronto, 1921.

William Bliss Carman was born in Fredericton, in New Brunswick on April 15th 1861. 'Bliss' was his mother's maiden name. She was descended from Daniel Bliss of Concord, Massachusetts, who was the great-grandfather to Ralph Waldo Emerson.

Carman was educated at Fredericton Collegiate School. Here, under the influence of the headmaster George Robert Parkin, he gained an appreciation of classical literature and was introduced to the poetry of many of the Pre-Raphaelites especially Dante Gabriel Rossetti and Algernon Charles Swinburne.

From here he graduated to the University of New Brunswick, obtaining his B.A. there in 1881. As is common with so many writers his first published piece was for the University magazine and for Carman that was in 1879.

England now beckoned and he spent a year at Oxford and then the University of Edinburgh (1882–1883). He returned home to Canada to work on his M.A. which he obtained from the University of New Brunswick in 1884.

Tragically his father died in January, 1885, followed by his mother in February of the following year. Carman now enrolled in Harvard University for a year. There he met and was part of a literary circle that included the American poet Richard Hovey, who would become his close friend, and later collaborator, on the successful Vagabondia poetry series. Carman and Hovey were members of the "Visionists" circle along with Herbert Copeland and F. Holland Day, who would later form the Boston publishing firm Copeland & Day and, in turn, launch Vagabondia.

After Harvard Carman briefly returned to Canada, but was back in Boston by February of 1890 saying "Boston is one of the few places where my critical education and tastes could be of any use to me in earning money. New York and London are about the only other places." However, he was unable to find work in Boston but was more successful in New York becoming the literary editor of the semi-religious New York Independent. There he helped Canadian poets get published and introduced them to a wider readership than they could receive in Canada.

However, Carman and work as an editor were not destined for a long career together and he was dismissed in 1892. There followed short stays with Current Literature, Cosmopolitan, The Chap-Book, and The Atlantic Monthly. Whilst these appointments provided the basis for a career and an income he was not suited to their demands. From 1895 he would only work as a contributor to magazines and newspapers whilst he worked on his volumes of poetry.

Carman first published a book of poetry in 1893 with Low Tide on Grand Pré. He had written the title poem in the summer of 1886 and it had (whilst he was still at Harvard) been published in the spring of 1887 by Atlantic Monthly. Despite its critical acceptance there was no Canadian company prepared to publish the volume. When an American company did so it went bankrupt. Life was becoming difficult for the young poet.

The following year was decidedly better. His partnership with Richard Hovey had given birth to Songs of Vagabondia and it was published by their friends at Copeland & Day. It was an immediate success. The young men were delighted at such a reception. It quickly sold out and was re-printed a number of times. Although these re-prints were small (usually 500-1000 copies) they were frequent.

On the back of this success they would write a further three volumes, which in their turn were almost as successful. They quickly became the center of a cult following, especially among students who empathized with the poetry's anti-materialistic themes, its celebration of personal freedom, and its glorification of comradeship."

The success of Songs of Vagabondia prompted the Boston firm, Stone & Kimball, to reissue Low Tide on Grand Pré and to hire Carman as the editor of its literary journal, The Chapbook. This ceased after a year when the company relocated and Carman expressed his desire to remain in Boston.

In 1885 Carman brought out Behind the Arras, a somewhat more serious and philosophical work centered on the premise of a long meditation using the speaker's house and its many rooms as a symbol of life and the choices to be made. However, the idea and its execution did not quite meld.

Signficantly, in 1896, Carman met Mrs Mary Perry King, who rapidly became patron, adviser and sometime lover. She put money in his pocket, and food in his mouth and, when he struck bottom, often repaired his confidence as well as helping to sell the work. She also later became his writing collaborator on two verse dramas.

Mitchell Kennerley, Carman's roommate wrote that, "On the rare occasions they had intimate relations they always advised me of by leaving a bunch of violets — Mary favorite flower — on the pillow of my bed." If her husband, Dr. King, knew of this arrangement he seems not to have objected. He was a great supporter of Carman's career and seemingly his wife's complicated involvement with that.

In 1897 Carman published Ballad of Lost Haven, a collection of poetry about the sea. Its notable poems include the macabre sea shanty, The Gravedigger. The following year, 1898, came By the Aurelian Wall, the title poem itself was an elegy to John Keats and the book a collection of formal elegies.

In 1899 his publisher, Lamson, Wolffe was taken over by the Boston firm of Small, Maynard & Co., who had also acquired the rights to Low Tide on Grand Pré. The copyrights to of his books were now held by one publisher and, in lieu of earnings, Carman took what would ultimately be a disastrous financial stake in the company.

As the century turned Carman was hard at work on what would eventually be a five-volume set of poetry; "Pans Pipes". Pan, the goat-god, was traditionally associated with poetry and the coming together of the earthly and the divine. The five volumes were all published between 1902 – 1905.

The inspiration for this came from Mary who had persuaded Carman to write in both prose and poetry about the ideas of 'unitrinianism.' This drew on the theories of François-Alexandre-Nicolas-Chéri Delsarte and was defined as a strategy of mind-body-spirit harmonization aimed at undoing the physical, psychological, and spiritual damage caused by urban modernity. The definition may be rather woolly but for Carman it resulted in some very fine work across the five-volume series. This shared belief between Mary and Carman created a further bond but did isolate him from his circle of friends.

The excellence of a number of these poems did much to install Carman as the most noted of Canadian Poets and eventually their own Poet Laureate. Among the most often quoted and printed are "The Dead Faun" (from Volume I), "Lord of My Heart's Elation" (Volume II) and many of the erotic poems from Volume III.

In the middle of publication in 1903, Small, Maynard failed and with it went all the assets Carman had tied up in the company.

Carman immediately signed with another Boston publisher, L.C. Page, who would publish seven new books of Carman poetry in this hectic period up to 1905. They released a further three books based on Carman's Transcript columns, and a prose work on Unitrinianism, The Making of Personality, that he'd written with Mary King.

Carman now felt secure enough to pursue his 'dream project,' namely a deluxe edition of his collected poetry to 1903. Page acquired the distribution rights on the condition that the book be sold privately, by subscription. Unfortunately, the demand wasn't there and it failed. Carman was deeply disappointed and lost faith in Page. However, their grip on his copyrights was absolute and sadly no further collected editions were to be published during his lifetime.

By 1904 his income was restricted and the offer to be editor-in-chief of the 10-volume project, The World's Best Poetry, was eagerly accepted.

For Carman perhaps his best years as a poet were now behind him. From 1908 he lived near the Kings' New Canaan, Connecticut, estate, that he named "Sunshine", or in the summer in a cabin in the Catskills, which he called "Moonshine."

With Literary tastes now moving away from what he could provide his income further dwindled and his health started to deteriorate.

In 1912 Carman published the final work in the Vagabondia series. Richard Hovey had died in 1900 and so this last work was purely his. It has a distinct elegiac tone as if remembering the past works themselves.

Although Carman was not politically active he did campaign during the World War One, as a member of the Vigilantes, who supported the American entry into the titanic struggle on the Allied side.

By 1920, Carman was impoverished and recovering from a near-fatal attack of tuberculosis. He returned to Canada and began to undertake a series of publicly successful and somewhat lucrative reading tours, saying "there is nothing worth talking of in book sales compared with reading. Breathless attention, crowded halls, and a strange, profound enthusiasm such as I never guessed could be,' he reported to a friend. 'And good thrifty money too. Think of it! An entirely new life for me, and I am the most surprised person in Canada.'"

On October 28th, 1921 Carman was honored at a dinner held by the newly-formed Canadian Authors' Association, at the Ritz Carlton Hotel in Montreal, where he was crowned Canada's Poet Laureate with a wreath of maple leaves.

Carman is placed among the Confederation Poets, a group that included his cousin, Charles G.D. Roberts, Archibald Lampman, and Duncan Campbell Scott. Carman was perhaps the best and is credited with the widest recognition. However, whilst the others carefully supplemented their income with writing novels and works for the magazines, or even other careers, Carman only wrote poetry together with a small amount of writing on literary ideas, philosophy, and aesthetics.

He continued his reading tours, and by 1925 had finally secured a new Canadian publisher; McClelland & Stewart (Toronto), who issued a collection of selected earlier verse and would now became his main publisher. Although they benefited from Carman's increased popularity and his revered position in Canadian literature, his former publisher L.C. Page would not relinquish its copyrights to his earlier works.

In his last years, Carman was a member of the Halifax literary and social set, The Song Fishermen and in 1927 he edited The Oxford Book of American Verse.

William Bliss Carman died of a brain hemorrhage, at the age of 68, in New Canaan on the 8th June, 1929. He was cremated in New Canaan and his ashes interred at Forest Hill Cemetery, Fredericton, with a national memorial service held at the Anglican cathedral there.

It was only a quarter of a century later, on May 13th, 1954, that a scarlet maple tree was planted at his graveside, to honour his request in the 1892 poem "The Grave-Tree":

Let me have a scarlet maple
For the grave-tree at my head,
With the quiet sun behind it,
In the years when I am dead.

Bliss Carman – A Concise Bibliography

Poetry Collections
Low Tide on Grand Pre: A Book of Lyrics (1893)
Songs from Vagabondia (1894)
A Seamark: A Threnody for Robert Louis Stevenson (1895)
Behind the Arras: A Book of the Unseen (1895)
More Songs from Vagabondia (1896)
Ballads of Lost Haven: A Book of the Sea (1897)
By the Aurelian Wall: And Other Elegies (1898)
A Winter Holiday (1899)
Last Songs from Vagabondia (1901)
Ballads and Lyrics (1902)
Ode on the Coronation of King Edward (1902)
Pipes of Pan: From the Book of Myths (1902)
Pipes of Pan: From the Green Book of the Bards (1903)
Pipes of Pan: Songs of the Sea Children (1904)
Pipes of Pan: Songs from a Northern Garden (1904)
Pipes of Pan: From the Book of Valentines (1905)
Sappho: One Hundred Lyrics (1904)
Poems (1905)
The Rough Rider: And Other Poems (1909)
A Painter's Holiday, and Other Poems (1911)
Echoes from Vagabondia (1912)

April Airs: A Book of New England Lyrics (1916)
The Man of The Marne: And Other Poems (1918)
The Vengeance of Noel Brassard: A Tale of the Acadian Expulsion (1919)
Far Horizons (1925)
Later Poems (1926)
Sanctuary: Sunshine House Sonnets (1929)
Wild Garden (1929)
Bliss Carman's Poems (1931)

Drama

Bliss Carman & Mary Perry King. Daughters of Dawn: A Lyrical Pageant of a Series of Historical Scenes for Presentation with Music and Dancing (1913)
Bliss Carman & Mary Perry King. Earth Deities: And Other Rhythmic Masques (1914)

Prose Collections
The Kinship of Nature (1904)
The Poetry of Life (1905)
The Friendship of Art (1908)
The Making of Personality (1908)
Talks on Poetry and Life; Being a Series of Five Lectures Delivered Before the University of Toronto, December 1925 (Speech). transcribed by Blanche Hume. 1926.
Bliss Carman's Scrap-Book: A Table of Contents (Pierce, Lorne, editor) (1931)

Editor
The World's Best Poetry (10 volumes) (1904)
The Oxford Book of American Verse (U.S. editor) (1927)
Carman, Bliss; Pierce, Lorne, editors (1935). Our Canadian Literature: Representative Verse, English and French.

9 781787 372108